To Nancy, Tracie, and all
the monarchs in Mexico, with love.
—T.R.

The editors would like to thank
BARBARA KIEFER, Ph.D.,
Charlotte S. Huck Professor of Children's Literature,
The Ohio State University, and
DR. DAVID GRIMALDI, Ph.D.,
Curator, Department of Entomology, American Museum of Natural History,
for their assistance in the preparation of this book.

First published in the UK by HarperCollins Children's Books in 2011
10
ISBN: 978-0-00-743308-7

Printed in China by RR Donnelley APS

MY, OH MY—
A BUTTERFLY!

by Tish Rabe

illustrated by Aristides Ruiz and Joe Mathieu

The Cat in the Hat's Learning Library®

HarperCollins *Children's Books*

I'm the Cat in the Hat.
If you look in the sky,
you might see a butterfly
fluttering by.

They are colourful insects
whose lives, you will see,
are very exciting.
Come on, follow me!

Right here out of doors,
if you look, you might spot
a butterfly egg.
It's a little round dot.

It sticks to a leaf.
Rain won't wash it away.
Right here on this leaf
is where it wants to stay.

You may think in these eggs
there are small butterflies.
But wait till they hatch
and you'll get a surprise.

Caterpillars hatch out
of a butterfly's eggs!
They look like small worms
and may have sixteen legs.

They start chewing and growing
and growing and chewing,
and that's about all that they
spend their time doing!

They eat first their eggshells.
Then it's leaves that they need.
They eat all the time,
and they grow with great speed.

If we grew as fast as they do—
this was funny to us—
in two weeks, we each would be
as big as a bus!

This caterpillar has grown
too big for its skin.
It needs bigger skin than
the skin it's been in.

So it takes a deep breath,
then it wobbles and wiggles.
Its skin starts to split
as it joggles and jiggles.

THIS IS
A SPOT
THAT LOOKS
LIKE AN EYE.

The old skin falls off,
and right there, underneath,
is new, bigger skin
that's been hiding beneath.

It eats the old skin.
(Oh, yum! How delicious!)
Protein in the skin
makes it very nutritious.

See this caterpillar?
He really looks cute,
dressed up in his new
black-and-orange-striped suit.

After the fourth time
it sheds all its skin,
the next stage of a
butterfly's life will begin.

It hangs upside down
like a small letter "j,"
and for a few hours
it hangs there that way.

Then it changes again.
The next stage is this—
a shell forms around it
called a chry-sa-lis.

CHRYSALIS

Inside the chrysalis
the caterpillar *keeps* changing.
All of its body parts
are rearranging.

For almost ten days
it can't move and can't eat.
Then one day
the butterfly's change is complete.

A tiny black leg
begins to poke through.
Within seconds, another
leg pops into view.

She bursts into the air!
A bright new butterfly!
Her wings are so soft
that at first she can't fly.

She must wait till they harden.
Till then, she must stay.
If an enemy comes,
she cannot fly away.

Her antennae start working
to sense what's around her—
the motions, the smells, and
the sights that surround her.

In hours, her new wings
get harder and so

she is ready to fly,
she is ready to go!

See these two caterpillars?
They're different. Here's why—
one will soon be a moth,
one a bright butterfly.

One makes a chrysalis,
and now we know
inside it a butterfly's
starting to grow.

PAINTED LADY
CATERPILLAR

CHRYSALIS

PAINTED LADY
BUTTERFLY

One spins a cocoon
like a blanket to hide it,
and then a new moth begins
growing inside it.

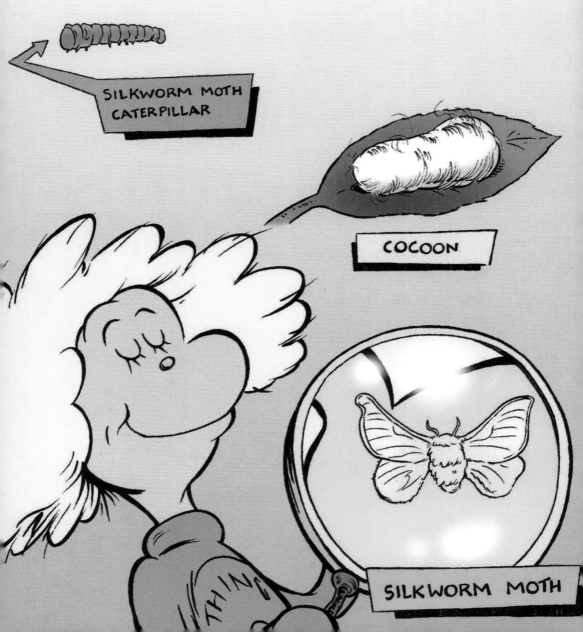

SILKWORM MOTH
CATERPILLAR

COCOON

SILKWORM MOTH

Spiders, frogs, beetles,
birds, lizards, and mice
think bright butterflies
for a snack are quite nice.

Every butterfly knows
birds are trying to catch it.
Its wobbly flight
makes it harder to snatch it!

Butterflies are so light.
This will show you how many
you will need just to equal
the weight of a penny.

They see thousands of pictures.
If one looked at me,

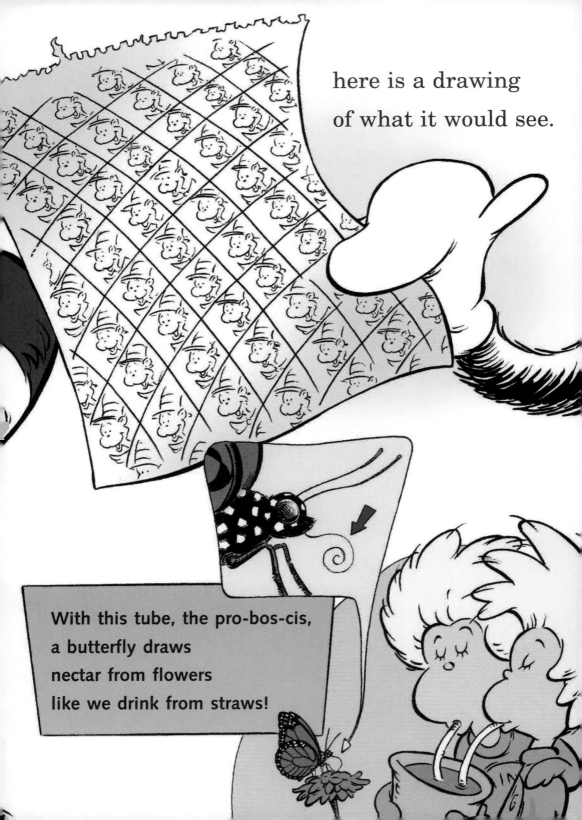

here is a drawing
of what it would see.

With this tube, the pro-bos-cis,
a butterfly draws
nectar from flowers
like we drink from straws!

We have a new hobby
we just started trying.
It's fun and it's free,
and it's called butterflying.

We look to find butterflies.
They're everywhere—
out of doors, near a stream,
on the ground, in the air.

PINE WHITE

MOURNING CLOAK

PAINTED LADY

We write down the day
and the time that we saw them.
We write down the place,
then take crayons and draw them.

Tiger Swallowtail

Red A

Tiger Swallowtail
FRIDAY 10 am   down by the
stream

Red A
FRIDA

CRAYONS

When you find butterflies,
there are ways you can see
by the size, shape, and colour
what kind they might be.

Butterflies get their names
from all different things.
Swallowtail butterflies have
long tails on their wings.

ZEBRA
SWALLOWTAIL

Here is a lacewing.
Its wings look like lace.

This owl butterfly
looks like a baby owl's face.

UNDERSIDE OF THE INSECT ▶

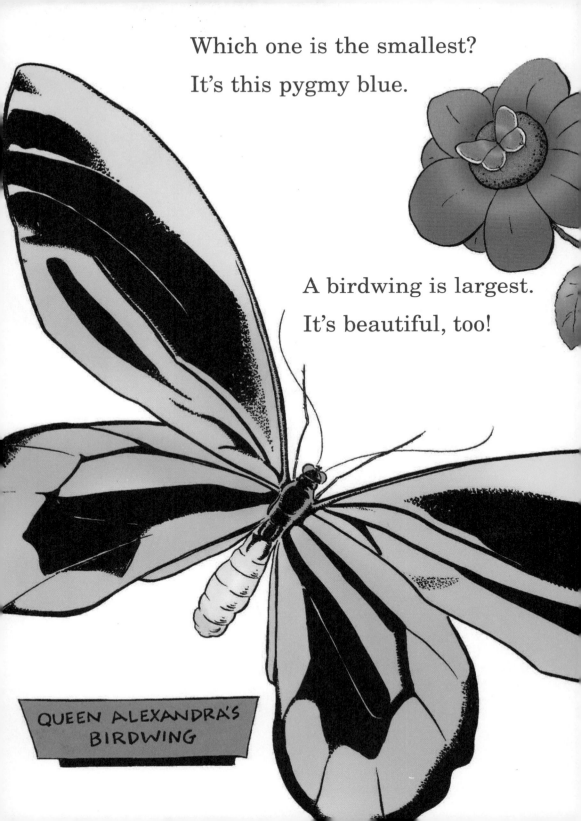

Which one is the smallest?
It's this pygmy blue.

A birdwing is largest.
It's beautiful, too!

QUEEN ALEXANDRA'S
BIRDWING

These are the monarchs.
Just watch them in flight!
They have orange and black wings
with small dots of white.

They can't live in cold weather,
so somehow they know
they must fly where it's warmer—
like to Mexico!

They fly hundreds of miles.

They fly hours and hours.

They stop just to rest

and sip nectar from flowers.

Monarchs hide in a storm
when the thunder is crashing.
They know they're in danger
when lightning is flashing.

How do these butterflies know where they're going? Scientists really have no way of knowing!

Butterflies can be tagged to show where they're from. This way we can learn how far they have come.

This one is from Maine, and I think this is cool— it was tagged by the kids at an elementary school!

Monarchs fly for weeks
till they finally see
in the Mexican forest
an oy-a-mel tree.

They fly to the tree,
and then just before dark,
they land and they hook
their small legs in the bark.

Without the sun's warmth
they are too cold for flight,
so they huddle together
to wait out the night.

Blow gently onto
a cold butterfly
and you'll help it warm up
so it's able to fly.

In the spring, when it's warm,
monarchs lift off from the trees.
They flutter and swoop
and they dance in the breeze.

Now that it's warmer,
these butterflies know
they must mate and lay eggs
so new babies can grow.

Males look for females
to mate with—it's true—
that have colours and markings
that look like theirs do.

Once a female has mated,

it's hard to go on.

She will not live much longer.

Her time's almost gone.

She is carrying eggs.
They are heavy. That's why
she cannot get back home.
It is too far to fly.

So she searches for leaves
and lays eggs, one by one.
She lays hundreds of eggs
and won't stop till she's done.

Butterflies are surprising
and beautiful things
as they soar through the air
on their bright-coloured wings.

They're like jewels in the sun.
They live just a short while,
but whenever you see one
you can't help but smile.

For you know, on a leaf
if you look you may find
an egg that a butterfly
just left behind.

And in this egg—
small as the head of a pin—
a new butterfly life
is about . . .

to begin.

GLOSSARY

Antennae: A pair of long feelers on the head, used to smell and to sense touch.

Chrysalis: A shell that surrounds a grown caterpillar while it changes into a butterfly.

Cocoon: A silky covering that a caterpillar builds around itself before it changes into a moth.

Foe: One who is unfriendly and ready to do harm to another.

Nectar: A sweet liquid found in many flowers.

Nutritious: Providing food necessary for life and growth.

Oyamel: A type of fir tree that grows in the Mexican forests that are the winter home of the monarch butterflies.

Proboscis: A tube-shaped mouth part used for sucking food or drink.

Protein: A substance found in all living things that is necessary to build and sustain them. Eggs, meat, fish, and beans are good sources of protein.

INDEX

If you love The Cat in the Hat then look out for these great titles to collect:

OH SAY CAN YOU SAY WHAT'S THE WEATHER TODAY

WOULD YOU RATHER BE A TADPOLE?

MY OH MY A BUTTERFLY

I CAN NAME 50 TREES TODAY

MILES AND MILES OF REPTILES

A GREAT DAY FOR PUP

CLAM-I-AM!

A WHALE OF A TALE!

THERE'S NO PLACE LIKE SPACE!

OH, THE PETS YOU CAN GET!

IF I RAN THE RAIN FOREST

INSIDE YOUR OUTSIDE!

FINE FEATHERED FRIENDS

OH, THE THINGS YOU CAN DO THAT ARE GOOD FOR YOU!

IS A CAMEL A MAMMAL?

WISH FOR A FISH

OH SAY CAN YOU SAY DI-NO-SAUR?

ON BEYOND BUGS

OH SAY CAN YOU SEED?